By Lingual Wholes

By Lingual Wholes

Victor Hernández Cruz

Momo's Press 1982 San Francisco

Some of these poems first appeared in *American Rag, Caliban, El Clutch y los Klinkies, The Face of Poetry, Maize, Mango, New World Journal, # Magazine, Quarry West,* and *Vortice,* and on the album *Readings at St. Mark's.*

Funding for this volume was made partially possible by grants from the National Endowment for the Arts, a Federal Agency, and the California Arts Council. Momo's Press is a project of Intersection, San Francisco.

Momo's Press
45 Sheridan Street
San Francisco, CA 94103

First edition

Library of Congress Cataloging in Publication Data

Cruz, Victor Hernandez, 1949–
BY LINGUAL WHOLES.

I. Title.
PS3553.R8B9 1982   811.54   82-8250

ISBN 0-917672-20-8
ISBN 0-917672-19-4 (pbk.)

The engraving on the title page is from *Cuban Counterpoint: Tobacco and Sugar,* by Fernando Ortiz, English edition published by Alfred A. Knopf, Inc., New York, 1940.
    The Chinua Achebe quote is from *Morning Yet on Creation Day,* Anchor Books, New York, 1976.
    The Abu Bakr Muhammed ibn Al Arabi quote is from *The Wisdom of The Prophets,* published by Beshara Publications, Gloucestershire, 1975.
    The Allan Kardec quote is from *El Libro de los Espiritus,* published by Stadium Corporation, New York, 1970.

In memory of
Don Arturo Vincench
who is on the other
side of the bridge
We will all come to
cross

The price a world language must be prepared to pay is submission to many different kinds of use. The African writer should aim to use English in a way that brings out his message best without altering the language to the extent that its value as a medium of international exchange will be lost. He should aim at fashioning out an English which is at once universal and able to carry his peculiar experience. I have in mind here the writer who has something new, something different to say. The nondescript writer has little to tell us, anyway, so he might as well tell it in conventional language and get it over with. If I may use an extravagant simile, he is like a man offering a small, nondescript routine sacrifice for which a chick, or less, will do. A serious writer must look for an animal whose blood can match the power of his offering.

—Chinua Achebe
Morning Yet on Creation Day, 1976

Now, as Reality is such as we have affirmed, know that thou art imagination and that all thou perceivest and that thou doth designate as "other than me" is imagination; for all existence is imagination in imagination (that is to say "subjective" or microcosmic imagination in an "objective" collective or macrocosmic imagination).

—Abu Bakr Muhammed ibn Al Arabi, 1165–1240 AD

Vuestro lenguaje es muy incompleto para expresar lo que esta fuera de vosotros; han sido necesarias comparaciones, y vosotros habeis tomado por realidades esas imagenes y figuras. Pero a medida que el hombre se ilustra, su pensamiento comprende las cosas que no puede expresar su lenguaje.

—Allan Kardec,
El Libro de los Espiritus, 1970

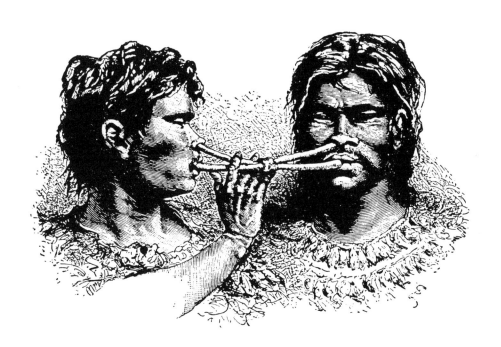

Contents

By Lingual Wholes

Habladera cambiando
a dentro de
espacio

Speech changing
within space

LA

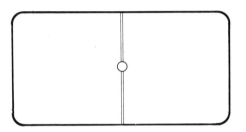

Anonymous

And if I lived in those olden times
With a funny name like Choicer or
Henry Howard, Earl of Surrey, what chimes!
I would spend my time in search of rhymes
Make sure the measurement termination surprise
In the court of kings snapping till woo sunrise
Plus always be using the words *alas* and *hath*
And not even knowing that that was my path
Just think on the Lower East Side of Manhattan
It would have been like living in satin
Alas! The projects hath not covered the river
Thou see-est vision to make thee quiver
Hath I been delivered to that "wildernesse"
So past
I would have been the last one in the
Dance to go
Taking note the minuet so slow
All admire my taste
Within thou *mambo* of much more haste.

Mountain Building

The mountains have changed to buildings
Is this hallway the inside of a stem
That has a rattling flower for a head,
Immense tree bark with roots made out of
Mailboxes?
In the vertical village moons fly out of
Apartment windows and though what you
See is a modern city
The mountain's guitars pluck inside
It's agriculture taking an elevator
Through urban caves which lead to
Paths underground They say Camuy
To Hutuado
Taino subground like the IRT in
constant motion

The streets take walks in your dark eyes
Seashell necklaces make music in the
Origin of silence
What are we stepping on? Pineapple
Fields frozen with snow
Concrete dirt later the rocks of the
Atlantic
The sculpture of the inner earth
Down there where you thought only worms
and unnamed crocodiles parade
Lefty stands on a corner
Analyzing every seed
Squeezing the walls as he passes
Through at the bottom of the basement
Where the boiler makes heat

The flesh arrives out of a hole
In the mountain that goes up like a
Green wall
Bodies come in making *maraca* sounds
An invisible map out of the flora
Bees arrive in the vicinity and sing
Chorus while woody woodpeckers make
Women out of trees and place flowers
On their heads
Waterfalls like Hurakan's faucets
Caress the back of Yuquiyu
God to all whose tongues have the
Arawak's echoes

Hallway of graffiti like the master
Cave drawings made by owls when they
Had hands
You see the fish with pyramids inside
Their stomachs
Hanging near the doorways where
San Lazaro turns the keys
Villa Manhattan
Breeze of saint juice made from
Coconuts
Slide down the stairs to your
Belly and like a hypnotized *guanabana*
You float down the street
And win all your hands at dominoes

The Moros live on the top floor eating
Roots and have a rooster on the roof
Africans import okra from the bodega
The Indians make a base of *guava*
On the first floor
The building is spinning itself into
a spiral of *salsa*
Heaven must be calling or the

Residents know the direction
Because there is an upward pull
If you rise too quickly from your seat
You might have to comb a spirit's
Hair
They float over the chimneys
Arrive through the smog
Appear through the plaster of Paris
It is the same people in the windowed
Mountains.

The Physics of Ochun

A group of professional
scientists
from Columbia University
heard that in an old
tenement apartment
occupied by a family
named González
a plaster-of-Paris
statue made in Rome
of Caridad del Cobre
started crying
The scientists
curious as they are
took a ride across
town to investigate
After stating their purpose
and their amazement
they were led to the
room where the statue was
Sure enough it was wet
under the eyes
Overnight, Señora González
told them, it had cried so
much that they were able
to collect a jar full of tears
The scientist almost knocked his
gold-rim glasses off his face
May we have this as a specimen
to study in our laboratory?
She agreed, and they took a taxi
with the jar to Columbia
They went directly to the lab

to put the tears through a
series of tests
They put a good amount of
the liquid under their
Strongest Microscope
Lo and behold!
What they saw made them loosen
their neckties
There inside the liquid
clearly made out through
the microscope was the
word: JEHOVAH
No matter how much they
moved the water they
kept getting the word
They sent for a bottle of
scotch
They served themselves in test tubes
They called the González family
to see if they could explain
All the González family knew
was that it was the tears
of Caridad del Cobre
They explained to Señora González
what was happening
She said that weirder than that
was the fact that her
window had grown a staircase
that went up beyond the clouds
She said she and her daughter
had gone up there to check it
out
because, she told them, a
long white rope had come out
of their belly buttons and some-
thing was pulling them up
What happened? the enthusiastic

scientists from Columbia University
wanted to know
We went up there and were
massaged by the wind
We got hair permanents
and our nails manicured
looking a purple red
My daughter says she saw
a woodpecker designing the
air
The scientists put the phone down
and their eyes orbited the room
We have to get out there
Incredible things are happening
They rushed back out
and into the González residency
They entered
It's in the same
room with the statue
They rushed in and went to the
window
So amazed were they
they lost their speech
All their organs migrated an inch
Clearly in front of them
a 3-foot-wide marble stair
which went up into the sky
The scientists gathered themselves
to the point of verbalizing again
They each wanted to make sure
that the other was "cognizant"
of the *espectacolo*
Once they settled upon reality
they decided that the urge to
explore was stronger than their
fears
One decided to take a writing pad

to take notes
One decided to take a test tube
in case he ran into substances
One decided to take a thermometer
and an air bag to collect atmosphere
Señora González, would you please
come up with us?
They wanted to know if she would
lead them up
If you could see it you could touch
it, she told them
She went out first and they
followed
The marble steps were cold
They could have been teeth of
the moon
As they went up the breeze smiled
against their ears
The murmur of the streets dimmed
They were climbing and climbing
when they felt a whirlpool in
the air
For sure it was the hairdresser
Señora González sensed the odor of
many flowers in the breeze
The scientist with the test tube
saw it get full of a white liquid
The scientist with the air bag
felt it change into a chunk of metal
The scientist with the writing pad
saw a language appear on it backwards
printing faster than a computer
The paper got hot like a piece of
burning wood
and he dropped it down into the
buildings
It went through an open window

and fell into a pot of red beans
A woman by the name Concepción was
cooking
Frightened she took it to a doctor's
appointment she had the next day
She showed it to the physician
who examined it
He thought it was the imprint
of flower petals
so even and bold in lilac
ink
The dream Concepción had during
the night came back to her
I know what's going on, doctor
I'll see you in nine months
Walking she remembered forgetting
to put the *calabaza* into the beans
and rushed home sparkling in
her yellow dress

For the Far-Out Experimental Writer

A woman is sitting reading a prayer,
her hands clasping the book on top
of a table
A yellow candle is lit
A glass of clear water is next to it
She reads the same prayer over and over
Other people in the room repeat and respond
to her prayers
Her voice starts to get drowsy
She starts to scratch the table
She is looking at the print but only
reads skipping paragraphs
She jumps up, throwing the chair across the room
She plants herself in the middle of the room
where her hands begin to fly in circles above
her head
Some of her neighbors are surrounding her
Almost everyone starts to burp
It's like burp burp
At once something took her and lifted her
so fast that she hit the ceiling
She broke the light bulb and came down with sparks
Now there was only darkness and the candles
Four of the people who were burping
began to spin and were slamming against
the walls
The other people who were not spinning
and not slamming against the walls
were looking for the people who were
One woman was shouting instructions

"Those of you who are circuits
try and make a connection
Plug yourselves in through the middle
fingers"
The original woman who was praying
was squirming and sliding through the
floor like a snake
Unexpectedly there was a knock at the
door
It was the North American man who was
known in the building as "el beatnik"
He was writing a novel and all the commotion
was arriving at his door
He was once in college but dropped out
to alter the state of prose
by using irregular time sequences
and adventurous typography
He stared inside and saw half the
people jumping up and down   broken glass every-
where   the candle lit   the glass of water
No one could tell him anything
and he never registered his complaint.

Art–This

Lucy Comancho is an artist
Art this
She makes all the stars in Hollywould
seem like flashlights which have
been left turned on for a week
She had a *frenisi*
A friend in C
A friendinme
with paintings and blowing things
up into color which came from nowhere
No one knows where she got these things
Her mother says too much thinking
She painted the walls in her house
She painted the hallways and stairs
the stoops the garbage can tops the
squares in the sidewalk the tar on the
street the plastic bags from the cleaners
the brown grocery bags the inside of milk
containers   She herself had to be contained
from painting your face the closest layer
of the sky elements everything she gave
brush to rush to paint your *nalgas* if you
gave her room She never thought of canvas
where they sell it absent from her view
Sometimes she was called Picassa feminizing
Picasso
She painted Josefina as I was writing
that Josefina is the feminine of José
Josés who are also known to go under the
nicknames of Cheos or Pepes and so
Josefina got tagged on her the name Pepa
which is female for Pepe and she dug that

Pepa for if you look close the other name
José *y fina* means José and thin or sounds
like *oficina* like Joseoffice also it had
something in it of José is *fina* José is
finis finished   no this for someone being
composed by an artis
To top it off Pepa also means *pit*
you see what is inside of fruits This
is all in Spanish and something is being
lost in the translation just like you lose
your natural color when you leave a tropical
country and come to a city where the sun
feels like it's constipated Ask Lucy Comancho
She knows about all this
art this
artis.

Listening to the Music of Arsenio Rodriguez Is Moving Closer to Knowledge

---

The researchers will come to
research the puddles of water
that we have turned into
all over your room

Doña Flores
who is next door
is not innocent
She too begins
to *liquidarse*

Warm water so good
Listen to the box
It is damaging
everybody

Opening like a curtain
the air in front of us
whistles
in the thousands of afternoons
that everybody is
nervously plucking
transformationally swimming
to where it is safe to dance
like flowers in the wind
who know no *bossordomos*

Inside your brains
each cell stands up
to *dance el son*
as the explorers come in
to research
yelling:
Where is everybody?
Are the windows opened?
Has it rained?

Tra-Verse

There is no need for you to say anything
My eyes are caressing your brain cells
Just sit down
Relax
and don't have any bad thoughts

El A Ve: Se   ENCY CLO PEDIA

A.

Which are the windows which I have
not seen any light in
Is there something that you
always miss
Do you feel funny sitting there
wondering what is around you:
Lizards   snakes   tigers
Flowers
plaster
Picture it maybe once professor.

B.

If sudddenly you had an eye
connected to you
Which was a mile above your head
You would see the buildings
The bridges   the rivers
Your neighbors
Horns   mirrors
Clouds
Jealousy and eyeballs flying
as needles
You would see the park of life
that bird's eye view
You see holes in your heads.

C.

Where you sit surrounded by
falling rocks you worship
The angel which led you to
the street.
Did you hear a drum made
out of your flesh
Maybe a frog has been
turned into a filing cabinet
All the folders have your name
you are paying tribute to
A sword being made in Toledo
For your head
lift yourself up
A wave of vapor
Comes this way
A sea of masks melting
Take it off: Azucar
Through the fog
visible now
Sharp teeth.

D.

A young woman from an Italian
Trapeze flying family
Sails between your ears
in the middle of your head
at 16 she has inherited
all the skills of her
Grandmother
All the turns
Spins
Jumps
Backward leaps
She is well balanced on the
String

E.

You see the bushes which are
on your path
Some will have to be cut
Others will require that
you make a comb out
of your ten fingers.
Most are decorations on the
corners
A sight to print   *cabezón*
Inside
The third cutting
is the one that has
the best completion

F.

Everything is time space and
molasses
So many windows moist from
thought and dance
Which are you parakeets of the
jungle
Do you keep my time
Do you know my favorite step

G.

Clouds remind you of shapes
you have seen walking
of words that have flown past
you all wet
While all your capacities
were anticipating
A television production
And you made like you were in
the audience

When her eyes were almost asleep
on the stage
Memory and imagination can
switch

H.

I bring you the truth of the
sweet and sour bones
As you look at a garden made
by possessed Japanese
Or a statue of gold
sculpted by Inca hands
The representation of
sensation
Manifest
Understand the vision of
the flowers with the neck
Look at one window
and open the rest.

La Milagrosa

As red as her lips were she wasn't there
The lonely night like a hidden moon crater
Which wouldn't be there if it were not for eyes
So look at the assembly of fire escapes
High up like on some kind of Ferris wheel
Hearing now footsteps inside the wax of the
Candle which burns for La Milagrosa
Go down the street to see *maniobras*
On the way back the gargoyle that protects
The entrance started talking:
The tops of heads have clear holes
I been spitting rainbows into them for
100 years tonight the half-baked moon
Is there I can breathe it with my nose
Which says the moon is full every day
All the time the moon is out and all
There full like your head in a dream
Close the windows
Aren't those the words of a song humming?
The street turns into soup
Her lips kiss the candle's fire
She walks open my walls
The sky is what I eat with my mouth
Virgin of the Miracles makes a
Sandwich of me between the sky
And the moon
Loneliness is yesterday's newspaper
She pokes her fingers into the silver
Holes of stars
Celestial orgasms like squeezing
Pluto-size cherries over a lemon earth
Roses clean their feet with the face

Of the gargoyle which looks onto the stoop
As red as her lips become blue
Like the mouth of an Alaskan glacier
La Milagrosa leaves footprints on my mind
She leaves stains on the goatskin drums
She leaves the odor of wax
She leaves the fire burning
She is gone from where she never came to
What you hear is only the song maker's
Humming
The street is deserted and covered with ice
The ice that used to be fire

To Much Imagination

If me and you did something
I would not tell anybody
On either side of the mountain
Would live my silence
Not a breath of it
Will be repeated after
The last breath I had
On you

I will peel you in my memory
Dressed blue blood
Nobody would know that we
Painted together that afternoon
That we made flowers
Ornaments—
Iberian perfumes
That we had two brushes
Dipped in a volcano
Lifting rocks looking
For fire: Purple

In a little room somewhere
A mat on the floor
Coconut oil—
A candle making shadows
Repetitions of the body
Movements
In the chamber where
The Indians shed their clothes
In no history will this
Be told
Nobody will know

That I seen you inside
Listen
Only you
Me
And the angels.

Layos

A Gang of Shorties

Sophisticated street where style erupts: some say slums
Those who cannot see will not hear the drums

§

She had the moon inside her mouth as silver teeth
If looks are transport her eyes were feet

§

She said it clear, betrayal cost more than seven
catholic churches
I sent her a letter: your voice is 3,000 miles away
and I am in heaven

§

Chocolate moving up and down marble stairs
puzzling numbers and sawing the zero, white souls
sticking out from their pockets

§

On the street
never associate one thing with what you see
standing next to it
Always walk around the corner

You can get involved with a dot
when you're high on some drug
A dot becomes everything in the world
A dot can appear bigger than a dot
Take heroin and look at a dot
till the dot massages your eyelids
Between the eye opened and the eye closed
your mental gear works with that dot
You think it's got a mouth, maybe some feet
What's dot doing up there?
You get convinced that the dot is a speaker
and you hear some music
Suddenly you realize your head is between your
knees
People who take acid can go inside a dot
Under the influence of cocaine one dot
would become seven dots
I saw a real coked-up guy take a broom inside
a dot, dust, paranoia written all over his face
Don't ever give a junkie a broom
In pursuit of debris he would redefine the
outline of the dot and go on further to make
a hole at the center
Coffee can make a dot appear where a dot
cannot be
The caffeine eyeball pretends to see a roach
on the distant wall every 2 minutes
How many times have you not slammed your hand
on the wall trying to hit a moving dot?
A dot can get into all the space in your head
In most cases just half a dot will do
After alcoholic beverages a dot is a friend
to you

You can see it as big as a garbage can
or sporting a mouth and giving you lip
Oh blabla oh blabla blu
Deep on mescaline you start to wonder
Could it be your own iris reproducing
outside your face?
This constant concern with a dot
can move you toward a rag
Once again don't ever give a junkie a rag
I've seen junkies clean whole buildings
going up and down the fire escapes
after dirt and falling into occasional dots
It is there where they show their expertise
They'll take a vacation in a dot
for those who didn't see a speck of dirt
will be amazed when they see this individual
come out with a sack
There are two kinds of dot maniacs:
those that see them on surfaces of walls or objects
and those that see them in the air with their eyes
open or closed
A dot is a madman's dream
'cause that means he's coming up on the
human airport
Habits all lead to this dot
Any habit
The habit of combing your hair
The habit of changing your clothes
3 or 4 times a day
The habit of wearing the same colored clothes
The habit of fidgeting with your hands
All that leads to dot
I myself have never seen a dot
but my report is based on firsthand
observation
I myself don't do dot
but I can point out a neudotical
3 blocks away

The Four Corners

The first corner has become a
bodega whose window is full of
platanos who have traveled
miles to rest in that reality
green with splashes of black
running down their spines
The other corner had a restaurant
a crab running out the door
speaking: You can't write about
my belly unless you taste it
The other third corner found
a group of friends singing
They became clocks with their
a zoon zoon zoon
zoon su Babare
The last and final corner
is where I stand
like a fool making this up

Juan (One) Village

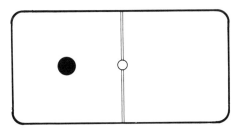

Two Guitars

Two guitars were left in a room all alone
They sat on different corners of the parlor
In this solitude they started talking to each other
My strings are tight and full of tears
The man who plays me has no heart
I have seen it leave out of his mouth
I have seen it melt out of his eyes
It dives into the pores of the earth
When they squeeze me tight I bring
Down the angels who live off the chorus
The trios singing loosen organs
With melodious screwdrivers
Sentiment comes off the hinges
Because a song is a mountain put into
Words and landscape is the feeling that
Enters something so big in the harmony
We are always in danger of blowing up
With passion
The other guitar:
In 1944 New York
When the Trio Los Panchos started
With Mexican & Puerto Rican birds
I am the one that one of them held
Tight   like a woman
Their throats gardenia gardens
An airport for dreams
I've been in theaters and *caberates*
I played in an apartment on 102nd street
After a baptism pregnant with women
The men flirted and were offered
Chicken soup
Echoes came out of hallways as if from caves

Someone is opening the door now
The two guitars hushed and there was a
Resonance in the air like what is left by
The last chord of a *bolero*

Don Arturo: A Story of Migration

A minimum of words, going through a maximum of time.
Dr. Mentelity Eson

Don Arturo has never been on an airplane. When he came from Cuba he took a boat; it was 1926. He had met a minister's wife in Habana, and she invited him to come and join her husband's touring musical Christian band in the States. Don Arturo thought about it for a few days.

He worked as an errand boy at the Habana Opera House; he had met Caruso and brought him coffee. He was around classical music in a tropical setting.

His family hailed from Valencia, Spain. His father played guitar, and Don Arturo picked it up like water down a dry throat. His brothers and sisters numbered 8, and he was the oldest. He helped raise them, and they had no money but they had a farm. They made food stretch like Jesus said to do.

Cuba was in turmoil and the economy was like a special delivery from the devil. The Guajiros rebelled coming down the mountains, angry like fighting roosters. He saw men shoot men with guns in the head; they fell down like sacks of rice.

When he was 18 he left the countryside to go to Habana to pursue being a priest. The priests in Cuba did what they wanted, including making love to the young women. Yes, my dear, confess your sins; they brought down skirts like peeling bananas. He got along with God but not with the church. When he couldn't take it any more, he left for the guitar and learned how to play the harmonica.

He jumped into Habana night life like a bee into a flower. The Opera House was full of stars and he mingled and got advice from them. He saw costumes, people rehearsing, and all kinds of instruments. It was like looking at a fairy tale.

The day he met the minister's wife, the *gringo* was asleep in his hotel room. She talked to Don Arturo like a woman on vacation, and Latins have the driver for the screw of metaphor. They made love on the beach that very night; like two animals they made a hole in the sand. He said she was wet like an orange.

He decided it would be a good idea to go the States with the minister and his wife. The minister met him and thought he was charming. They got on a boat, all three, and watched the lights of Habana get eaten by the ocean as the boat moved along to New York. He got his own private room on the ship, and since the food was part of the service he kept it coming. He got stuffed like a bed bug in a hotel.

After midnight the minister's wife would knock on his door. She sliced in like a sheet of paper and told him her husband had fallen asleep with the Bible on his face. He started talking to her in Spanish, which she half understood, but the warmer she got the more she comprehended. They took advantage of the boat's natural sway. She left for her husband's room before daybreak. Her husband commented over breakfast that the food was better on the boat than in Cuba. Arturo said that better than the food was the soul of Christ.

The boat blew its horns when the lights of New York appeared on the horizon. Arturo looked at it and thought it was a stage in a *caberate* getting ready for the night show. It was summertime, and the weather was warm like in Cuba. Some people from the church were on land waiting for the ministerial couple, which now included Don Arturo and his wicker suitcase.

They drove to a small apartment building that was attached to the minister's church on the lower west side of Manhattan. They gave Arturo his own room and keys and he went up to take a nap; he dreamt about boats coming out of fruits and whales that became guitars and Siboney Indians hanging dead from rosary beads. They knocked on his door to see if he wanted dinner. He went down to join them, and the beef stew was orbiting the Bibles.

The minister and his wife sat next to each other as they introduced Arturo to the other people present, three women and two men who were members of the traveling band. The minister spoke of the purpose of Arturo, his fine guitar playing, and where he could fit in. One of the women informed them all that they would rehearse the following day. The food became invisible like the Holy Spirit.

After dinner Arturo excused himself and said he wanted to go out and look at buildings. To him it was another world, something out of a picture. At first he walked as if the street would cave in under him; he looked at the structures and then went up to them and touched them. He made his way to West 14th street where he began to see Spanish-speaking people and Argentinian and Spanish restaurants featuring seafood.

He saw a Catholic church that was old looking and reminded him of the ones he had seen in pictures of Mexico. When he got close he saw that it was called La Virgin de Guadalupe and was truly fashioned like the Spanish churches of old Mexico. He entered and blessed himself with the cool water that was at the entrance.

After contemplation he marched out into the hot sun. He entered a restaurant and sat down to order coffee. He noticed that the Argentinian waiter spoke a different Spanish than his; it was as if the man hissed at the end of his words. A young woman sat at a table next to him and he started chirping to her like a bird. She joined him and opened up like a fan from Granada.

She told him her father was a merchant seaman stationed in New York. She had come to live with him when her mother passed away in Buenos Aires a couple of years back. She told him that the West 14th, 15th, 16th, and 17th streets area was a section where Spaniards and Latin Americans were settling. They talked through two cups of coffee. Finally she invited him to her place and he said yes four times.

The apartment was a railroad flat which she shared with her father who was at the moment out at sea. It was handsomely fixed up with furniture and gadgets from around the world. A picture which had dried butterflies from Brazil hung on one of the walls. A new Iranian rug was on the floor.

Arturo got taken by her beauty and forgot all about the minister and his wife. He played with her eyes and she smiled from the interior. He asked if he could touch her tongue and she shot it out like a cash register drawer. He squeezed it and asked if she had come from Venus. She said that she had arrived from there that very day. This drove him crazy and he went for her buttons.

Arturo got glimpses of the minister and his wife waiting for him and wondering how he was making out in the big metropolis. He thought of what he should do: should he stay the night with the sweet Argentinian rose or track through the dark streets? They fell onto the rug tied together with arms and legs and rolled from one side of the parlor to the other. He fell asleep, his face on her neck. They awoke and chatted. Well, he had to get back. He explained the whole church situation. He left after they arranged to meet the next day at the same restaurant for lunch.

She was golden heaven, and his mind heard trumpets. Angels played harp as he walked back retracing his path. He found the church and with his own keys entered and went up to his room. He fell onto his bed like a piece of lumber. It is this way that Don Arturo had his first full day in the USA.

With the minister's traveling band he went in and out of cities and towns saving souls. The Depression was on the horizon. Meat had to stretch like rubber bands.

Arturo was an expert at survival. He got tired of plucking wire for the Christian band and massaging the minister's wife. Soon he found his own furnished room in what is now Spanish Harlem; the neighborhood was populated by Germans, Spaniards, and Cubans. On 3rd avenue there were cigar-making shops (*Chin-Chals*). He knew Mr. Bustelo when he was getting his coffee beans together. He knew the Valencia family when they had plans to spread their sweetness as the biggest Latin bakery of wedding and birthday cakes in New York City.

When the market crashed he became a street musician taking a position outside Macy's and sometimes Gimbel's. He played many instruments at the same time, even putting a tambourine on his feet. He sang popular Latin American songs and told jokes. Sometimes he got arrested and he put puppet shows on in the courtroom. The court clerks rolled on the floor.

The manager of Macy's toy department took a liking to his entertainment qualities and hired him to sell puppets and give floor shows inside. Winters came over him like layers of blankets. His hair started to get like pepper that was sprinkled with salt.

As a street musician he began performing in a spot in Greenwich Village. Tired of commuting downtown he moved to the Lower East Side.

Now 78, he still cultivates his famous corner in the Village come Spring and Summer. He savors memory like espresso coffee. He calls up his beautiful moments with women like an encyclopedia, though his memory sometimes scatters. The details he gives shine like light bulbs and make bridges with each other.

Together we sit and talk, staring at the abandoned buildings of 10th street where inside doors are still intact and the hinges are lonely for motion. We review time and its fibers. Sipping on white German wine we both chuckle at life's contradictions. Always spice it with laughter. Remember too much insisting can break even iron. The lights of the building go off and we light two candles and sip in the darkness. His hair shines like white threads of silk.

Don Arturo recognizes the old refrain: All of life is a hole. How so? The man enters the woman's vagina, which can be described as a hole; the infant, you come of this very hole; you eat food through the hole of your mouth; you breathe through the holes of your nose; you shit through that famous hole; and when you die they drop the total you into a hole in the ground. So you see, all of life is a holy hole. Bet hard on that.

The wine which is sweet and old comes out of the hole located at the top of the bottle. We laugh ourselves through the linoleum, me and Don Arturo, who is 78 and to this day has never been on an airplane. The way he got here the story you have been told.

The Process of Bolero

Pushing a big heart through a small
pen is not difficult
Through a six-string guitar
the heart comes out red first
It is followed by the rest
of the organs
In the love song tradition
which says it is better
For the one that leaves
than for the one who stays
One follows a sigh
The other swims in tears
Your heart is an oven
and a generation puts their
Cookies in it
They say the furnace has
its windows in the eyes
In the songs of love
the heart comes through the
mouth
It is followed by the whole
body
Your soul jumps next through
your throat
making holes in the air
        burning up pages

"Put Seeds into the *Maraca*
So That It Could Sound"

Ironing Goatskin

The air is suffocating
In the altar which is the sky
The sun the only statue
On this beach the vibrations
Of the drums
The fat barrels of the Bomba
The Papa, the Mama, and the Niño
The way the sound goes up
Your head goes seaward on *canucas*
Listen
Mercy for the goat flesh, please
The drummers look at the
Mahogany legs of the girls
Who enter the round Bomba circle
And proceed to imitate them
Turning the visual into sound
There isn't a place to sit your
Lungs down
It is for this reason
That we should be concerned
With the destiny of goats.

Merenque in History

In the 18 hundreds a law was passed by the colonial government
of Puerto Rico banning the dance *merenque* among the population
of the island. The dance rhythm is as fast as a drum can go; it
vibrates more than a mambo by about 30 percent. If you were
caught dancing it with your girl friend, lover, or a perfect stranger,
they took you to the capital, San Juan, to give your accounts.
Favorite punishment was to attach you to huge wooden wheel on
the uppermost deck of the Morro (Spanish fortress protecting San
Juan) and slowly roast you in the sun, as if you were in a modern
Bar B Que Pit. It was a slow arduous process, a very slow legal
dance with the sun. Much slower than the *bolero*, the ballade, the
fish, the grind, it was about 100 percent less vibrant than the
original crime.

    Make no mistake, there must have been a spy informing
authorities as to the change in rhythms. Let's see how would they
know it wasn't a *plena*, or even a *meranque* danced like a
plena. Ponce de León knew that to be truly successful he'd have to
ban feet. His persecussiveness attitudes came back in the form of a
Florida search for youth, first suggestion of encloning. The other
thing they were doing was colonizisation. Today the *meranque* is a
big craze on Broadway, and back then, as like right now, you
could always walk into the mountains and enjoy yourself.

Here Is an Ear
Hear Hear

Is the ocean really inside seashells
or is it all in your mind?—Pichon de la Once

Behold and soak like a sponge.
I have discovered that the island of Puerto Rico
is the ears of Saru-Saru, a poet reputed to have lived
in Atlantis. On the day that the water kissed and
embraced and filled all the holes of that giant
missing link, this bard's curiosity was the greatest
for he kept swimming and listening for causes.
He picked up rocks before they sank and blew
wind viciously into them. Finally he blew so hard
into a rock that he busted his ear drums; angry,
he recited poems as he tried turning into a bird
to fly to green Brazil. His left ear opened up
like a canal and a rock lodged in it. Rock attracts
rock and many rocks attached to this rock. It got
like a rocket. His ear stayed with it in a horizontal
position. Finally after so many generations he got
to hear what he most wanted: the sounds made by flowers
as they stretched into the light. Behold, I have
discovered that the island of Puerto Rico is the
ears of Saru-Saru.

Prescriptions from the Plantnet

When they prepare to find the answer to what has been asked them, they eat an herb called cohoba, *either ground or ready to be ground, and they inhale the smoke of it through their nostrils, and this makes them go out of their mind and see visions. When the power and properties of the herb have worn off, they regain their senses. They tell what they have seen and heard in their council with the gods, and say that God's will will be done.*

—Francisco Lopez de Gomara, *Historia General de las Indias*

The Mint Family–*Yerba Buena*

If your stomach starts to come to your brain, go hunting for this scent. From the pores outside your nervous system will come stage lights. Makes your bowels like a Pacific ship. You'll hear the stems converted to flutes. The night wraps you in a blue haze.

Albaca

To go toward a cow by a river where women sit by the edges banging clothes on rocks, only you will not see any of this for you are the fish.

Pasote

One step at a time you enter the veins of the leaf, you enter a slide where your feet are worth nothing. Down this funnel you are going like water in a tube. The passage puts you on the other side of flesh or an eyeball coming out of a cliff.

Patchouli

At the bottom of an old Spanish trunk I found patchouli because the odor preserves the thread that must survive through time. Perfume for your closets or tropical mothballs.

Mejorana

Mejor que Ana, Nada.

Anamu

Depending on which part of the branch you pick up, one side has a monster called Umanasata; the other has a princess, La Ana of Mu. Oh, the art of bending down.

Rompe Saraquey

Entrevu into that head; what you realize is that you didn't need it. It also breaks Saras crab.

Yerba Bruja

Take your nose off, take your ears off, take your eyes out, unscrew your skull, place it in a pot and boil; she will come in a beautiful green robe and drink you but she will throw out the juice witch is which.

Ruta

If you get stuck on the route, call Rota-Ruta to flush you out; then you see clearly a pipe with seven keys and a tribe of feathers behind you.

Yerba Luisa

A girl named Luisa sits on the grass. To meet her you'd have to take a bath. Down your back she will slide. When you come out you will never see grass again, and Luisa will have nowhere to sit. This is the beginning of imagination.

Sofrocoton

Comes from the blue trees abundant on Jajuya road leading into Good Waters. Fry this leaf with eucaliptino twigs and rub on any pain, but never eat the fruits of this tree, for they are too high to reach, and if they fall they are too ripe to eat.

Almistris

Take down from branch with left hand on first Wednesday of any month; otherwise, it will work in reverse. It will make you see the color blue as green: the sky would look like an avocado and you like a mouth that's eating the truth.

Alta Misa

A mass celebrated in a land higher than the Andes. Your organs will have sensations of being vertical in heaven's line while your skeleton sits in a nightclub where the juke box was invented.

Borete

Great for eliminating stains like those caused by green bananas.

Salvia

If your molar was extracted by the town nut impersonating a dentist, place this leaf on the space and the bleeding will stop, like turning an industrial switch.

Malva

Boil it with cloth rags. Put those rags over any pain. Before it leaves it shellacs the bones. Your flesh feels like it's pressed against ball bearings. Next time you ache, take Malva.

Satosoti

Weird, because after you pull it off the branch it keeps jumping like a jumping bean. Sometimes you got to hit it with something; any object of good weight will do. When it gets down to its thing it has no comparison; it is an anti-dizziness drug.

Tobacco

Anesthesia. Immediate delivery to any wound of the flesh to halt its bleeding. Smoke to blow away earaches. Nicotinia to rid your house of mosquitos. Cable for the phone calls of the mediums.

Lemon Tree Leaves and Flor Tilo

If your nerves have gone haywire from too much thinking of ideal situations that never materialize, drink some tea out of this plant and you settle down almost into a nod. The world could blow up but you tranquil.

Guarapo de Maquey

Tired of your blood? Send a broom down into it. Sweep up all the bad particles. You'll be like a whistle. A drink of this could have saved Ponce de Léon instead of giving him that run around.

Flor de Roble

Goodbye, Dr. Scholls. You put this leaf on your corns and pop corn.

Mala Madre

In Shakespearian it is known as spider plant. You take the leaves and dry them. Later boil the tea out of them. If you have any grease this will be for you; grease will dissolve like addicts at the arrival of narcos.

Fideillo

So fierce that as it grows out of the ground it chokes neighboring plants. It doesn't care; it could be a sweet rose. Some things out here can also kill; that's why you can't be so happy-go-lucky. Something can crawl up your leg and choke you. It could be your last botanical kick.

Puerto Rican Joke Riddle Told in English

Can he take the *Can*.

Geography of the
Trinity Corona

Galicia Gypsy tongue sucks salt water
Red fish *gitana de* Galicia
Sings
Romany *de* Hindus
Romany *de* Hindus
Ibericos boats from the soul
Boats from Ibericos lust
Schizophrenic ships search golden dust
Ladinos
Ladinos
Ancient Spanish
Ancient Spanish
Lengua del Kabala
Kabala *lengua*
O Mohamet *flor del este*
Flor este del Mohamet
Sonrisa of same people
Flor de Maya
Lengua primordial agua y sal
Mora eyes of paradise
Gypsy freeway
Gypsy freeway
Mohamet
Ladinos
Romany *de* Hindus
Valencia
Where sound parked in the tongue
Galicia *con pan*
Pan Galicia
Pan pan Ibericos

Bridge made of white handkerchiefs
To the cascabells of Andalusia
Walking light the on the loose
Gone through the strings of sitars
Guitars / Sitars
My strings are here
A si
Cadiz   *camara* my friends
In the pupils   of time
Jump barefoot into the circle dance
Here comes the Romanies
Islamicals
The Rock of Gibraltar
Rock of Tarik
Like the wave of the ocean
After retreat
On the sand it leaves pearls
From the bottom
Shaped like three-dimensional mandalas

Take my boat
Take my boat

Gallegos *gitanos*
Jump the Arawaks
The *michicas*
Who had gold like we have the air
Golden halos
Of Maya Cocos
Tainos skidding through
Carib sea on canoes
Church pierced the mountain
Gallelocos everywhere
Cement came down from heaven
Taino areyto echoes from the flora
Gone through the pipe of time
Into the face

Into the cheek so cute
Espana danza
Africoco bembe
Burundanga mixture is the word
Bembe Mohamet   *Areyto*
Layered peacock cake
Sandwich of language

Take my boat
Take my boat

Yoruba *y* Arare
Lucumi
Cascabels of Romany gypsies
Nativo antillano
Hindus
Gallegos
Africano
Caribe
Rythmic circle
The islands are beads
of a necklace
Tarot cards with tobacco smoke
Crescent moon
The handshake of Fatima
Golden and red hot rubies
Chains where sacraments hang
Symphony of
Moorish flamenco
Fans opening like sound
Out of the acoustic mama bass
Streets of Islam wrapped in
Catholic robes
Where they say an eye for an eye
Teeth for teeth
Jump for jump

Make my Spanish lamp
Make my Spanish lamp
Walk the camels into the gardens
Electric flowers
See them shine
Make my Indian time
Make my Indian time
Song is memory
Memory is song
Take my boat
Take my boat
Make my African alphabet
Skin on skin
Make my African alphabet
Skin on skin

Mohamet Africaos
Look the street is full of
Ethiopians
Look Jersey City full of
Tainos
Gitanos *lindos*
Lucumi inside Yucaye
White angels come from
Arare drums
Visual spectacle envied
by rainbow
Look Pakistani mambo
The ears are the musical race
Even polish my Polish
Mazurka in the *guava* villages
Blood vessels of combined chemistry
From everywhere to someone
Galicia
Romany *de* Hindus
Arawaki
Arare

Moro
Lucumi
Ibericos
Mohammedans
Gypsy
Arabiscus
Yoruba
Tainos
Colors turn into sounds
We start building cities
From blueprints
Found in the sails
Of remember

Take my boat
Take my boat

Bacalao and Society

Cod fish thinks underwater
The Portuguese tend to go after it
In the form of dry cod it was the
food of the exploration voyages
Surrounded by salt the first currency
it stayed ready each day more salty
But once in the pot hot water can
debate it and portions of it leave
Everything 'cept milk can be put
into it
Swift net Portugales
on the dish
on the coast
live on wood atop the liquid
after the cod salt
Flaboyante   Catholic dances
Roman apparel for the building
For wedding or baptism
fry cod or boil it
onions or tomato sauce
Event the height of tears
The whole palette a furnace
where *bacalao* melts
The whole street an orange dream
Where she walks
and where for she he walks
The lowered house white on blue
heaven
The smell of *bacalao ala* Vizcaina
makes your head also turn
Eyes push open a curtain
Music escapes every time a salt

pebble divides in half
For cooking long hours you need time
and songs which hum within you
Your finger tips are mouths
so stubborn when it goes into the
hot water
It comes out shaky and loose
spreading apart into layers
The finger is warm from hot water
and clean from lemon
The thumb should press what you
consider to be the head of each
piece
It breaks in half with edges of
fiber
Your relation to a sea
or a mountain determines what
you put around it
The Portuguese got all parts of
the world
Outside a million things
inside one word for it
They divided tribes for domination
Like a big octopus whose arms did
reverse after touching fire
It went back into itself
They go fishing like looking for gods
Back home to sun falling wine
In Bahia   Rio Piedras, Camaquey to rum
the favorite and most coquette
Tune is Bacalao ala serenade.

Perlas

---

pa José Fuentes

The old men in the hills
say they shake the bottles of rum
to see if they have any pearls
They are bubbles that speak of the spirits
The longer they last
the better your drink
Good pearls will make you whirl, they insist
The earth is not straight
so why look at it that way?
If you walk on the beach late at night
The waves will not get you dizzy
if the spirits have your sight
Sunrise will find a string of pearls
around your head
Good rum must have pearls
That is good knowledge
That is something that you need

Ocupación-Información

Vamos a sabor de donde viene el
café y las flores
Ojos hacen percha de tierra
Sos etiopios estudioses árabes
tan alertos que se desaparecen
Los petalos son del centro de la
nube.
El bolero sube
Tu tristaza de café.
Esperan palabras detrás
del algodón   molestoso
Dos manos   viran una
montaña patas arriba
Hacen un baso y
Beben jugo de tabaco
Cada dedo sueña
los sueños   de las generaciones
Pasadas
Ojos de ajo miran con duda
pero hay que entender
Lo que entienden las piedras.
El mar esta lleno de peces
que no conocen la realidad mojada

El siglo 19 no se acaballado
ni se a bañado del siglo 18
Por eso la habladera pesa
Cabezas enbeleque y también
tembleque
En la plaza sesos
Porfian sin información
Guindao en una jamasca

un clavo en cada idioma
Paloma le lleva nota al
pescao
Que hizo espejuelos
de agua y oyó el gran
Salmon Información en una
cabeza y en otra es un color
Son dos personas
adentro de un yo-yo.

En la distancia oigo
los espetardos del revolu
Sera un sabado en San Juan
donde la policía canta
Son las trés de la macana
vamonos
Tanta gente que cultivan
el lenguaje gofeta
Son una carcel donde nunca vino
el amor
Su casa muebles sin corazon

Programas
Políticas
Ideas
Construcciones
Ingredientes
Literaturitas
Vamos a usar lo que trabaja
y lo que no
A votarlo al safacon

No tropiesen con palabras
Las letras son arboles en tu camino

Hay que vivir con un gobierno
Todo gobierno esconde un infierno

Estudien lo que nunca han visto
la mariposa economica
Alas para todos imaginar
libros   experiencia esperitistas
La ciencía oculta
Hay tantos enchufles
Confunden mucho cuando
a los telegramos
Le meten su propio arroz
Si tienes dudas
Dale una flor a Buda
También una fruta ajuda
Pero sique tu técnica
Información es sabrosura.

A Tale Told by the Tongue of a Shoe

Zapato walks with his shoes on
the good *lomas* stepping on nobodies
Shells hiding the confused standard
Transmissions and batteries within
Cigar leaves he makes lyric tobacco
For the seventy mouths of his shoes
Trees lit with kerosene lamps
Help him see on the stroll
Velvet thrown over mountain
See them curve
Memory the shower you take
Rent an apartment in Caracol
He lives off the soul of sole
When he takes his walk asleep
Into those 9 street longs
Refreshed he doesn't want to
Play the game
Go into his shoe
Into his glove Wilson / Wilson
The lungs benefit his walk
Two trombones golden like symbol
Zapato skips through lying truth
Mad at mad he doesn't want to dance
Not even if Maria takes him out
Not even if a star drops on his
Lapel
Not even if the afternoon was
A sun made to stand still cause
Someone hammered it with a nail
Something you can step on

Like a zillion Bazooka gums
On a street near the equator
Will make you stop importing
Dreams from Colombia
Only the white-eyed *cumbia*
Books like 100 years of solidness
From town to town the Page goes
With the scroll his stroll
Looking for a spot
Where he could gaze on being
Shoes
That can walk away and start
Again the factory of leather

If Chickens Could Talk

This is the story of the men who stole chicken soup after it was properly made by others. The odor was walking up the stairs, and they heard it clearly, and something inside of them said to them from the very inside of them that they could go and get it with maneuvers properly laid out, quietly, sneakingly, no creaks from boards. Old buildings have a silent motion toward death.

Some cities invent ways of keeping them going but this does not matter to chicken-soup-hungry men who are friends and have drunk two, three, four, or (1) (2) (3) (4) beers together or two shots of rum or three glasses of brandy and / or one bottle of California wine. They were sitting around involved in this process, just waiting to be presented in their proper setting in a state of minding their own business busyness, mining their thoughts deep into prehistory, times when they didn't do the same as now, though possibly the smell of chicken would have maliced their day / afternoon / night—especially from an open window, an opened mountain, a dark valley with crickets inventing gossip, a river's eternal flow creeping through the elevators and punch cards and glass.

In this case they actually knew where Buena Parte got the chicken, alive, three blocks down, one hill over, six songs away, across one river, two roads, one car, one horse that didn't break its iron wheels industrial age turning subway. He walked down the street with the beautiful chicken and the populace wondered, Fried / boiled / fricasse I *no se* I no said *Ay no say* can you see the wings flapping? Something in the blood or where the genes remember telling the chicken also from deep inside that it was going to be denecked expertly by Buena Parte, who paid good money for the chicken, and the men were already drinking slowly to commemorate the clock's large hand going on to the three going on two the tree and Buena Parte even saluted. It was perfectly the same shape as it is implied. No rough edges in his even

wave of his hands and lips saying, "Hello, *buenas dias*," and asking
to Big Mario, "Thank you, God." That "to" does not mean two
Marios, because the world would have to deal double accordingly.
Such a perfect encounter between all the elements who are all friends.

Once Buena Parte is off vision the friends served themselves
another, and their minds began to skate fulling or filling or feeling
with theories as to the destiny of one tall chicken whom they all
know now belonged to Buena Parte, who was a champion at
snapping chicken throats and was constantly commissioned by
neighbors who now dwell in the interior of his Memorex. He
went up the stairs. Chicken is called *gallina* in Spain, Mexico,
Puerto Rico, El Salvador, Nicaragua, and 14th street. The stairs
are conscious of his stroll; after years of contact it could not be any
other way. He has fallen down them and they have not moved an
inch to save his delicate parts. They are cruel stairs, who add extra
escalóns as the years go by. They enlarge and make your destination
appear farther.

"What a fine healthy chicken," his neighbor Doña Entretodo
tells him as she greets him from her doorway where moments
earlier she was not there but was perfectly inside wondering if she
should come out and when and greet and how and solely to dis-
cover / find out / register exactly what was the commotion that
she saw from her window as she saw with her eyes, the same ones
she uses to sleep, what went down with Buena Parte and
something in motion within his hands as he marched past the
friends who were jolly, curious. Buena Parte didn't suspect any-
thing and was only thinking about carrots / potatoes / onion /
green peppers / garlic / salt and all that *that* that that he will
always put all ways in the chicken soup soup, after he shaved it
and offered three feathers to Santa Marta, after he opened its belly
and stuck his fingers in it and took the belly out and cleaned it
with hot running water inside / out and then took a green lime
and cleaned and scrubbed the walls of the interior chicken and
began a system by which the total chicken became parts, and
parts, pieces. After that a formula of dropping it into the *olla*, each
ingredient having a cue for entering and dissolving / embracing /
jumping / rubbing / composing its perfume, which spilled out

through the pictures of swords and the bread that was hanging over the doorway scaring away the devils of this or any world, so potent the grace that it filled the hearts of men with envy and desire.

When the chicken was an empty space Buena Parte went downstairs to the world, and he sang like a chicken and said, "Does Buena Parte taste good?"

The Swans' Book

In my neighborhood I saw two swans take a taxi
because they got bored of the mirror they had them in
Year in and year out they bought flowers in front of them
The mirror reflected the red the orange but the swans
couldn't touch the blues   so they got bored like
an unfound book in an abandoned building in the
South Bronx
One swan said to the other:
Who are these hypocrites who have parties and
throw rum in our faces?
They look like coffee percolators with their
excitement
We can't live, only look at it
I want outs, I'm gonna unglue off of this heated
sand and make for the door
I agree, said the other swan, and they peeled
off the glass mirror from the corner where
they decorated   spread their white wings once
and out the door they swayed
Each floor they passed had a different smell
Like one floor smelled sweet like bananas
The next one smelled like tamarind
The next one like incense
They marched past the people on the stoop
who in a state of shock froze like winter snow
You see things in the world, one said
A pedestrian looked so deep his eyes went out of
his face like on wheels
But the swans were into their thing
and that corner was for them like cake from
the oven and if they saw the owner of the
mirror they'd tell him where it was at
To hell with living motionless
suffering nonproblems having delusions

worrying about everything
just pressed against a wall that belongs to
a landlord who never comes in the winter to
understand cold
Watching people dance, all kinds of formations
Every rhythm gots a dance
People eat white beans and don't offer
The odors were killing us
To hell with being the swans decorating the
right-hand corners of mirrors
Everyone says how beautiful we look
and then ignores us like some inanimate object
Lulu to those who will see the blank we leave
behind
Now that we gone the city will turn gray
The residents will fight
from seeing too much nothing sitting next to each other
We don't want to be microphones for someone who
combs their hair with Dixie Peach and sings tragic
bolero blues about broken hearts and impossible loves
while a toothpick hangs from their mouth
That's right, that it is, gasoline with this place
On the corner they flopped their wings
A big taxi came to them
They sailed in like keys into a lock
When the taxi sped away from the neighborhood
one wing came out of each of the side windows
The crowd that mingled noticed the swans
escape
The yellow metal elevated into the air
dwindling into a dot
as the residents chit chat about the spectacle
One of them pops:
Now it's our turn to wake up
A loud voice was heard in the eardrum
Hey, wake up
before that mirror falls on your head

Two Tongues and
Some Green Bananas

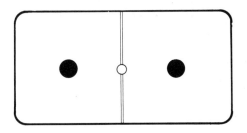

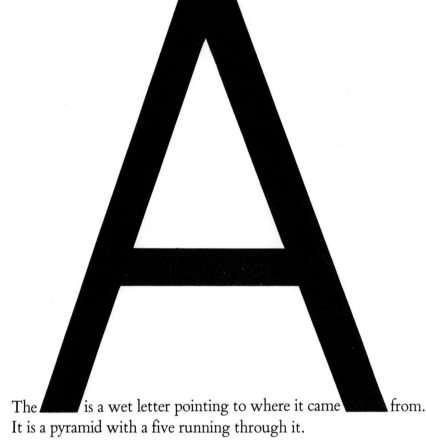

The is a wet letter pointing to where it came from. It is a pyramid with a five running through it.

La  es una letra mojada señalando hacia el cielo su origin.
Es un piramide atravesado por un cinco.

La Ley: Luz con Luz, Loco al Loco

Consuelo llego al piso.

Table of Contents

Your tablet is your inner workings, your grasp on the board, which is shifting, trying to knock the items balanced on the table kitchen or desk, motion *contestivis* of accumulated objects. Objectivity too is matter of this piece of wood. A *tabla* is in the dictionary, transporting itself like: *tabla* (1) *(de madera)* of wood: if you lose this you lose grip as implied in conversation somewhere like Rio Piedras, Puerto Rico; (2) *(de metal)* sheets: moments among buildings, big structures, boats, autos, irons ironing your skull base for greater irony; (3) *(de piedra)* slab: also chunk of reality, let's say a piece of voice not knowing its pretty qualities are being used beyond its own life; (4) *(de tierra)* strip: episode which should be recalled right in the strip; this feels like going through distance back to a time that was slowly being eaten by this moment when it is still trying to hold onto the table; (5) *(cuadro pintado en una tabla)*: situation which has been thoroughly explained into your metabolism or a framework, something that works within a frame of four sides painted clearly so you can distinguish shapes, and *contenido* reversed means *nest contained*. This is a list of tables. Broken legs will lose the tablet, and you will place your fingers on the wrong weather. Whether you at the time thought perfect your box of index, this tablature will accurately give you all the stops on a road for which you have an unsccured map with inscriptions and designs.

Let us not lose our table as we praise the importance of its acquisition. So the flow goes that it is also a catalogue *catalogo— cadaloco* means each crazy one of all the material involved. Such a list is the one you have to have faith in to maintain your tables analogous to your mind health. This wealth leads to a Spanish *(table de lavar)* wash table where the surgeons reconstruct dilapidated jungles inside of your vision from which they (this) move you (to a *tabla de planchar*) and stretch you out (to *tabla de salvación*), at which point you might have capreached and you would (*tener tablas*) to present your presence on a stage to the world and bad light would not harm you. Tablear cuts you into pieces, separates you into patches / streams / numbers / notes till you level to approachable grade for tabletear signifies to rattle, ultimately, realizations that a table has four legs and within it contains space, unless it is the table of multiplication, whereupon you will see everything in doubles or substance folded. Tabloid stretched out has many stories that are placed one by the other into pictures and features done so you can continue to follow your interests and arrange them in your pocket neatly like a well-versed drum alphabetizing names of peoples and whereabouts of mountains visible and under earth. Figures pop into your *tabula rasa*, empty where there is no grease or *grasa*, a simple search for *gracia* gracing this directory which has given deep tales and details of detours so we may come to a *principio* or principles. Let us now table this tablederia of context tabled.

Confusion

A moth
landed on
his hand

He immediately
saw
that it had
4,269 specks
of dust on
its wings

The Map Inside

Wood would have been the first would be
His what is what made what what what is

The water it shines at night by fluorescence
The hot natural waters to bathe in south

Caves with echoes and this symbol
At the entrance to where further down you want

Turtles are now coming out fingertips
Caress coral red like her lips

Copper to make you a heaven
You count ten, I count Yucatan

With Yuquiyu eating Yucca
And José inside of Cuca

Off that peninsula which is oblong square
Is the beginning of Cubism

Now that's the hardest cookie
Brown and rectangular

You're not lost
Fly cool with woody woodpecker

A pawnshop under the rocks
Sings in blues

How would you like to be clay
Or twenty feet tall?

The stars like fire on the ceiling
When they shoot they lecture your curls

That avenue of bronze and leaves
Corn cooking juicy with fish

Soul pushing out of tamarind husk
Coffee in coconut shell, it's all lost

Flowers frozen in ice waiting for sol-light
Music lost out of seashells

Turns the motion of the islands
On a head   backward to a map

The Appearance of *Cucubanos*

(Fireflies)

Bi-Lingual Education

When things divide
the nature of this age
like 12 midnight when heaven
and hell slice
don't look in the mirror
lest you see yourself
your tongue hanging out
like a carpet
where two ladies
are sprawled   entwined
They come to eat you
in doubles
They chew you
till you are
a strong and perfect 1.

Ver-
sion   cíon

EACH LITTLE	CADA
PORE	PORO
HAS A LIGHT	TIENE UNA LUZ
AND OUTSIDE	Y AFUERA
DARKNESS	OSCURIDAD
YOU SHINE	TU BRILLAS
ONE HALF	UNA MIDAD
GREEN	VERDE
THE OTHER	Y LA OTRA
BLUE	AZUL
WHAT A PICTURE	QUE PELICULA
LAND	TIERRA
THAT	QUE
JUMPS OUT	BRINCA DEL
THE WATER	AGUA
SALT COMES OUT	SALE SAL
OUT OF YOUR	DE TUS
BONES	HUESOS
TO MAKE	PARA HACER
MEAT	CARNE
WITH AIR	CON AIRE
LIKE POCKETS	COMO BOLSILLOS
WITH MATCHES	CON FOSFOROS
INSIDE	ADENTRO

Hearing Inside Out

O uno habla con las cosas
O se esconde de ellas
y ellas hablan solas

The translation through
a rear view mirror

Things the with talk one her either
Alone talk hers—and plus

The Organs of Speech

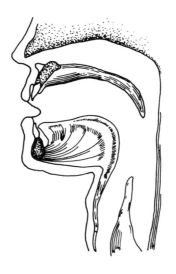

Haikukoos

City News 1

Wallet in pocket
Money stuffed like burrito
Look!   gone man slices wind

City News 2

Into self-service
Elevator he goes smooth
Bang!   now stuck he hums

Legislator Sheet

Government talk shit
Then file it in office jobs
Everyone flushed

Andalusian Thought

Skirt of silk music
Woman sits back in darkness
Wait!   Is she naked?

City News 3

All morning he heard
Screwdriver making hall sounds
Mailbox!   now he thinks

Movement of Molasses

Men argue honor
While twenty blocks away their
Women train horsies

Textile

She wear the pants red-
dish and tight what is under-
neath nature hills fly

Iota

A roach from Colom-
bia has enough legs and
walks the ocean back

Tree with Routes Everywhere

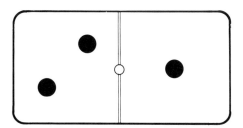

Groenburgewal Straat

para Steef Davidson *y* Gea Stadig,
Dutch *divinadores*

Three ducks in caravan sail by
On the canal which swallows street
The street swallows water and feet
Old buildings leaning from the
Weight of the sky

Cold makes your mind be a boat
in the Carib sea
Ducks with buds in water
Stride with brushes on their beaks
Free from shivers and this
Radiator heat

Paint themselves hanging at
The Rysk Museum next to bread
and wine
Lunch is on the walls
Guards patrol make sure
You don't bring spoon or knife

It seems that a Dutch Master
Insulted a passing man
The man went home and got a
Blade
He cut one and punched another
Out
The others ran for muskets

Amsterdam is round like a
Pancake

Streets make hooks   loops
And circles into each other
They seem to rotate
Whole sections relocate
On the streets Indonesian
Jade
Percolating out of Edam cheese
Curaçao coconut bridge
Colonialism is always
Take and get
Energy colonizes the cream

The sounds of gongs
Announce the coming
Down a canal of
The craftsmen of the
Ancient Pacific boats
The inventors of paper
Rice fingers
Bells which unite
With streams in the blood
Awake the people

The moon is a round
Gouda
Its dress is the water
That circulates
The ancient village

Where everyone is always
Recreating on bicycles
Light blasting out
of red hair

This constant merry-go-round
Ah, where is this
Amsterdamn?

Grafo-Mundo

para Adál Maldonado

Mi fuzz era en aquella era con la radiola televisión cuando su luz
lumbraba to la cosa del wallesque llegaban suburbos de pequeños
pueblos de paraisos Califononos donde ahora se ve que la proble-
matica también existe pero ante eran los sueños de los vecinos no
vencidos por tantos mar de ojos como compañias que se ivan con
el dinero y si no asi también se iva el dinero esa cosa que va y viene
siempre que lleque primero para luego poder irse pues ahora yo
tendré que formar una formación thema de paredes donde vinó
el hilo electrico a transformar teniendo un número atomico mayor
las paredes sembradas paredes cortas   venian shows o
chows   edificios altos que se van por hasta que se acaba el cielo
paredes de gentes estucish entro el espaciosolitos que los dejó la
vida buena la vida mala las realidades de mosaico de colores las
costumbres de tiempo España molestando el soquisoqui
metropolitano y tampoco importa el lenguaje de metaje tantos
verbos y adjetivos que?   La luz visual vino entrocada en una caja
de madera de palo viejo no el cantaso que te liquida sino el que
crece entro la selva Electricandolos de cosas que aparasan en la vida
de las moferas Uno se olvidaba de la temperatura de cuando
empeso el frío y se iva uno pa Califonia a correr en carros en coches
lindos blancos y sueves coetes en problemas no problemas como los
cristales que tosian hielo pa dentro tu cama que por casualidad sola-
mente cabia en esa parte del cuarto pero eso ehta en la memoria
que los siquiatra dicen esta parquiá en la sección Hippocampus del
seso eso un caballo que va recordando por debajo del agua   Tam-
bien un club en el Bronx debajo del tren pa guarachar   Pero lo
más serio era el fuzzyses del radio-localizada alla en el principio de
nueva vista ciudad entre medio del agua: Aquas Buenas y eso que el
televisor cogía solamente 2 canales en uno por la mañana empieza
gente a llegar a materializar en aviones y bombitas con caras de
payasos Entran brincando con la asucar más dulce del mundo esas
camaras que estan detras de los montes y valles esplotandose salien-
dole hamburger y catshotup   Que visiosos la gente televizionada

nunca tendran tranquilidad siempre que pasa algo pasa por el rinconsito en el cuarto con el ojo abierto al mundo estran-fancado de dolores y a la gente eso le da risa pero ya tengó la misa para su rapido cambio de colores los espanta como pajaros para otras islas Cuando el día estaba verde todavía salía un hombre gordo con animales de tierras perdidas estrafanos salían winstikees parecían no se a Pascofe olían a hijo de Migeta resemblaban en el Sabado tan temprano que se podía smeller la noche en el cuadro metío en el cuarto cuadrados todos los motocos.

¿Quien fué que trajó aquella caja?

Tenía puertas y botones tenía volumen y un programa con un hombre jugando con unas bolitas que tenían numeros metías en una caja también otra caja con un aire que las hacía bailar y con eso el ambiente pasaba el tiempo con la lucha libre con aparatos rellenos de libras expertos en recibir dolor Apagaban la caja y avía baile en la sala   Apagaban la caja y avía   soles en las caras cuando bailan se dan gustos los elementos Gusto no se donde pero gusto como risa que hace más risa un colder de risa era por esa era que le dava gusto a uno por to los laos creo que era gratis el gusto que le dava al señor la caja del album de alegría se parava y informava los dedos y los pies con los tubos de los ojos enshuflao to los días gusto cosquilla es lo que pasaba sonando toda cabeza abriendo las puertas del verano gusto del invierno (sin piel no) gusto de las saciones do las canciones brincando en un disco su cosa te da ya gusto tu ve y tu gusteas eso sonando no parando también como el piano mira algo tan lejos sorprende cuando llega desde alla y analiza la tranquilidad cada fibra desde aqui hasta ya   entra tus pisotasos molestando el tuquitu con todos los mecanicos afilando piesas areglando preguntas decorando hasta el arroz y afuera las niñas lindas   pasaban parecían la historia andando por las calles davan gusto de primer grado a la mirada Y el disco lo dice serio también "si se rompe se compone" Pero la caja duro tres inviernos hasta que no pudo más y es tres que no es guitarra cubana por poco llego al cuatro guitarra Puertoriqueña   y casi to lo que hablaba era en esa era en Ingles se rebala mucho en ese idioma y solo porque un recuerdo vinó   no solo porque tenía miedo presentarse si no en las caras de aquellas que pasaron   Que-que tu no ves que estan escondidas detras las paginas detras las cajas   Es así que yo me recuerdo y sigo pasando este Grafo-Mundo.

Translation:

Grafo-Mundo: Graphic World. Picture it.

Esplendoriendote, Aun

A soft movement for your memory
glistening legs   powder cinnamon
or white
something shiny like wood rubbed
with cream
all softly united like the idea
of a *danza* a *danzon* not calvary
music exciting a football
Softly and like a frog
squeak if you wanna squeak
Scratch me gently
My forehead
inside like a foto color
projector
in tradition and out of it
is called the fountainhead
where you receive evidence
Scratch it there to see yourself
while I eat your eyebrows
Don't frown or be crazy
Light a candle in the four corners
if you want
slowly and clearly
sight arrested by your

Nothing can stop the curve

of me and you jumping
making sense
tonight
In California coconut trees
without coconuts
fall and break sweetly
It's oil that I rub into your
question mark in English
And in Spanish the question
comes upside down and is found
entering the sentence and leaving
it at the end

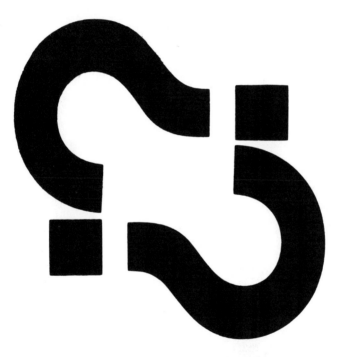

Dolores Street

Through the Victorians
spinning a wool of music
the gang in the breeze
Boys and girls headed toward the
park
No longer in my view
Wondering now what they doing
How they divide
Hold hands
Lay on benches
Breathe

Dolores park green waving
mounds
where downtown looks like you
could stretch and scratch it
You can see the water
smaller the other side
connected with the bay bridge
from this angle
Appears as a cowboy rope
Lasso

Back to the park
the across the street is windows
Suggest
Eyes which could have been looking
at savannahs / stretches
had it not been for transportation
The city settling
Up from planks and kerosense lamps
Rugged

Small vocabularies full of passion
Found a gold sliver on the way
to my fruits
Raise the air fair
Let the news out
Rush like Hawaiian beer

The big radio of the teenagers
comes again
looking through the curtain
Look them wasted
Clothes wrinkled
Eyes fresh like just arrived mushrooms
they move to the interior of the Mission
where they hang out / generations on the streets

Pupusa

Pink,
la motion
wave flesh
mahogany
silk and blue
Buttons flying
opening
like a Salvadorian
pupusa
Enter *cultivo*
The salad
in the finger
changes gear
stuck all the
way A musical
pipe delivers
each
unfolding
skin Yellow
corn in there
The spider
knows
what it
weaves
Pink motion
la silk
The eyes open
like the
gates of heaven
mandalas
in orbit
with fingers
eating *pupusas*

The Low Writers

Who first in the human planet invented the wheel, its use as transport, now see it someone caressing a mountain watching rocks and pebbles rolling, coming to a stop in front of their toes, just picture, gee, if we were ants clinging, or something more minute unnamed creatures of the tropical berserk, an orange pin head moving with eight legs, the ancients must have said how quickly this carries it through the terrain. Now the first hatch back would have been inside rocks, or in the dream to be a pelota flying through a Taino park, send a message which travels distance and I can catch it with my fingers.

Out here puffing, jamming, moving down boulevard, deep into the industry of tires, red wheels, blue tires, metal sunk low around it, like a closed eye or a blink, constructions floating, home made interiors, Roman Chariots dodging, trunks full of batteries. In Peru the llama was freight carrier over through mountains paths whose history they were starting, for gasoline they gave them Chicha and coca leaves, zoom through streams, atop where it's cold down to the hot flatlands, edges of towns where they traded woven blankets and disappeared into the clouds. And that petro took them through sky tree branches, the llama white and bushy, serene, a caravan of miniature camels.

When I am in this room that flies it is as if I invented rubber. Like San Jose Low riders interiors, fluffy sit back, unwind, tattoo on left hand, near the big thumb a cross with four sticks flying, emphasizing its radiance, further up the arm skeletons, fat blue lines, Huichol designs on the copper flesh, the arm of the daddy-o on the automatic stick. A beautiful metal box which many call home. It doesn't matter if the manufacturer was Ford or General Motors, their executives in the suburbs of Detroit watching home movies, vacationing in weird Londons, when the metal is yours you put your mark on it, buying something is only the first step, what you do to it is your name, your history of angles, your exaggeration, your mad paint for the grand scope of humanity, the urbanites will see them like butterflies with transmissions. Take it to Mexico and get a round figure to the maniacs of Tijuana, who break it down to slices, throw it back together, slice it up again.

Once a circus caravan of riders from Watsonville took twenty cars down, puffing and flying and bouncing all the way; only stopped twice by Highway Patrol, but they looked so looney, that the officers perhaps behind a beer or two, let them go, saying this can't be real, plus they were clean as a Mormon in Salt Lake City, license and registrations, and hydraulics well hidden.

Zoom, all enroute toward TJ to get their interiors layed out, they know who to see, one tall Tony, another guy called Gordo, talk right adjust your price, Tigar, Zebra, velvet, polka dots, colors your dream, shit never heard of, tugged in tight, last you a century, you go before your car will, blazing stuff shag rug pink running across dashboard.

Twenty cars rolling, eating the road from here to Tijuana, from here to Tia Juana, music from the Pioneers. All the mozos some with mozas sporting lumberjack shirts, leaning, brown hands, the tattoo cross where Christ was tortured, on the steering wheel cutting edges, a mosaic of tongues rattling, can we say unidentified flying objects, private discos, patterns, a piece here and a piece there, if that don't work enter the garage of spare parts.

Mission Street is El Camino Real, is the old road of Christianity, if you start riding from 24th you could go in a straight line all the way to the gates of gold. From path to road from road to street to avenue from avenue to boulevard from boulevard to airport from airport continue to space station, looking for those white crystals, don't kid yourself the Northern proposition has always been vertical, an uptown kind of motion, towards the mechanics who lay out your interior, how real is the Camino, El Camino Irreal where car junkies glide into the southern and northern lights.

The scene on the road must be here comes Ali-baba and his twenty machines, going South to get to their North. But wait, how long will this oil supply last. 2050, you cannot replace it like coffee or tobacco, Columbian oil gives its own seeds, but the blood of the earth once it's taken out leaves space. Do you figure they will be able to equip motors with new gadgets that will allow them to digest an alternate source of energy, *si no, se acabo la Honda*. The whole landscape will be full of rust, only the low riders pleasure boats will be assigned to museums. Tony blows: And my hand against that dashboard, in my studio roving, dazzling right below the mini charro hat swinging from the rear view mirror, with its embroidery in gold and silver, gold rings you bunch of susus, exhibit relaxation, the State of California made the roads for us, the princesses in shiny cabins.

Who invented wheels, invented roads, but movement which is before avenues, before circles invented itself, it made enough of itself to be available to all, to be interpreted according to each, its like you enter and perform, like the full fleet of twenty cars riding towards TJ will each have its own coat, their common language is their closeness to the ground, they want to kiss the earth, they want to penetrate the many disguises of their mama land, have we been in touch with you are we rubbing you right, to be on this road is this the way we say love dangling from a window driving Smokey Robinson and the Miracles, OoooooBaby, Baby OoooooooBabyBaby, green light go, stop light red stop, yellow light put your feet down tight, in the hot rod land what can we do with our hands but attack the steel, mold it, make it unique, each will be different for the same purpose.

Hector blows: When my cacharro goes down there's not even room to stick a nickle in at the bottom. The steering wheel is the handle of measurement, skinny ones, made of silver chains, prisoner chains, industrial chains, smoking chains, the smaller steering wheels allows for quick jerky precise turns, tricks that only road runner could perform, beep beep, make room for the modern car yachts of the Watsonville Road Kings, monarchs of the boulevards, never bored always going somewhere, now enroute south, towards, the land of the articulate mechanics, who work with their eyes closed and create short of putting a toilet in the back. A style of craftsmanship, concentration, it features remnants of a classical point of view, the car is the living room, like Gothic mixed with Toltecas, my space to freak you out, come delight in my red peach fuzz sofas, enjoy the stereo sound from my Pioneer speakers, picture the chrome hanging like a painting in a gallery, car club emblems showing through the back windows: Watson-ville Road Kings, jumping and moving, cleaning the surface, when the gasoline stops pumping the vehicles will run on perfume and music.

Keeping Track of
the Serpents

This is what will happen
This is what will go down
This is what you been thinking about
What last night's dream was planting
This is what has been written
By drops of water at the tips of tree roots
This is what you been trying to decipher
This is the secret of the rocks
This is it:

Near the center of the earth
Circulate huge reptilian snakes
The size of the Lexington Avenue
Subway Express
Thousands of them
With faces the size of cars
Amazing
Add to that the fact that
Their faces are human
And their hair neatly combed
In a twist

Their appearance is what's going
To go down next
Wham! no matter where you live
Eating pork chop in a slum
Or caviar in Hollywood hills
When you see it your eyes will be
In Cartoonland
As they pop to where these

creatures surface
In the commotion that will
Follow
Some will run for their dictionaries
Others will go for their zoological books
Many will go for their Bibles
Since taking pictures with cameras is in
You can imagine the rush for the film
The churches will be packed
As will be the offices of scientists
Talking about
We must get a hold of it
We must name it
It's gonna be like wow name that shit
The military will go for their heat

But wait
This is what has been written
This is what's in the tablets
Endlessly and has come down to this
Shock which has popped
This huge snake with a cute old face
An hour or more after their appearance
The legend starts churning
Not only do they dive in and out the
Water with their strips of primary colors
They zoom off into the air
And start to orbit clouds
The scientists munch on their brains
The christians are confessing like birds
The air gets full of flute sounds ˎ
Above the snakes like gypsy scarfs
Spinning washing machine the air
Colors are fruits for the eyeball
Mouth

It's all over, some say

Even the hustlers give up their
Circle
This has got to be it
No the phenomenon keeps weaving
The huge flying snakes
Turn the sun off and everything is
Black until they turn their lights on
And they are moving rainbows
Now get a hold
Even your feet start to dream
That the sidewalks commence to
Dance and wax the whole earth up
Like a glass
This human-faced snake
Next starts to excremetize
Greenish pink bubbles
Coming down on your head
To shampoo your pendants

As it was written that it will
Manifest itself
When this number 56,979 will talk
As it is in the codices
As it is known in the stars
What the waves of the ocean scribble
This is what will happen
This is what will go down
This is it

Cinco de Maya —

The Greek Theater
in Berkeley
Gets full like a
Bowl
Corn-maidens
Barley princesses
Rye toast
Wave their spring
Bushies
At Zeus-Apollo
As the singers are
Them
What's come to be
From the mouth
The meter
DEMETER
Pluto's rope
Lassoes at the
Various *personificadas*

The eyes are gloves
Baseball flowers

La Voice filters
Shango sprayers
The air
Plumed serpent
Circles this
Egg-shaped zero
Springs all
Motherflethers

Amphitheater
Musically 3 beats
2 beats clave lawyer
Oval *pelota* going
Toward everybodie's
Top head Sun
Hang on to your
Round *platos*

Dance and touch
The hands
Of distance
Sweet *contemplato*
From afar
Syrup in the
Fruit bowl
Inside

Plato knew the
Sun was here
This gorgeous
Theater
Of his people

THEOS-CALLI

Borinkins In Hawaii

For Norma Carr, Blaise Sosa
And Ayala and his famous corner

In 1900
A ship left San Juan Harbor
Full of migrant workers
Of the fields
Enroute to what they believed
To be California
Instead something like C&H
Which managed the vessel
With strings like a puppet
From afar
Took them to Hawaii

When Toño who was one of them
And Jaime who was another
And Felipe who was a third
Of the many 8,000 who took
This spin
Saw Hawaii they thought they
Were still in Puerto Rico
It took movement of time
Show up of the wind
It took the Japanese currents
To convince them
That in somewhere they were

Sugar was the daddy on the
Commercial horizon
Donuts for everybody
Ah history was getting sweet
If you wasn't a cane worker

With sores on your feet
And corns on your hands
Under the sun for how much
A day
Sugar was gonna blow flesh up
Sugar mania
Sugar come from cane
Get some cane
Get some workers
Get some land

The United States talked to the
Old Hawaiian queen
It was a polite conversation
The gringo merely pointed
To where the Marines
Were casually placed
Just that
The Hawaiian Kingdom
Pieces of cake
Littered on the Pacific

"What in the mountain got
Into you Toño to wanna come
From where you were
To jump on this boat
To come to this other planet.
Looka a volcano to lite your
Cigar, a desert for your
Camel, what is this the
End of the world, HA."

"Well Jaime look a guava
And coconut is coconut
See that tree where a Pana
Hangs. Smell the flowers
Fragrance like Aguas Buenas."

Thru each Pana-pen a metropopis
Of juices and texture
Ulus are Pana-pens in Puerto Rico
Ulus:Hawaii
Pana-pen: Puerto Rico
Breadfruit for you
Ulus hang like earrings
From the ears of women
On the tree
A blue dress on top
The curve is the horizon
A reminder that we all live
On a Pana-pen

Hawaii fuedal 19th century
Catholic liturgy
Thru the flower tops
The best years of
Tomas-Toñon
Jaime
Felipe and the full migration
Living in camps
Box homes for workers
And their families
Early risers
Church on Sunday
Machcte on Monday
Orange curtains thru
The greenery
Cuatro strings
With the bird speech
The pick pickers of
Pineapple stress the
Decima
As back in Borinkin
Ya se men
In ten lines you hem

A skirt
In Kohala they call it
Cachy-cachy
People jumpy-jumpy
Like roosters
The cuatro guitar chirps
Squeeky its note in the
Upper C high nose pitch
Sound of the Arowak
Garganta of the Areyto
Song gallery of the
Ancient inhabitants
Of the boat Borinkin

Broken guitars navigating
Vessels
Arrive like seed onto the
Ground
Whatever is in the dirt
Will come out
We're gonna finger pop
The pineapple
The cane is gonna fly
The mayordomos will whip
Ankles
Secret hidden wood
Will get them
There are dark passages of night
Roads under the kona trees
In the dark the sound kaploosh
On the skull
The mayordomos are paid
By the plantation owners
The wood is made by nature

At Ayalas Place
3rd & 4th generation Puerto Rican

Hawaiian
Eat rice and beans prepared
By Japanese woman
Soya sauce on the tables
Hawaii only Puerto Rican
Oriental community in the
World

A ship which left San Juan
Turn of the century
Transported workers music
And song
They thought they were
California bound
But were hijacked by
Corporate agriculture
Once they got to land
They folded over
`They grew and mixed
Like Hawaii can mix
Portuguese sausage slit
Inside banana leaf
Filipino Japanese eyes
Stare from mulatto faces

The Portuguese brought
The ukulele to anxious fingers
Who looked at the motion of
Palm leaves to help them search
For a sound
They studied the designs of
The hula dancers
And made
A guitar which sounds like
It's being played by the
Fingers of the breeze

They all dance cachy cachy
And jumpy-jumpy
In places like Hilo
And Kohala
You hear the shouts
You hear the groans
You feel the wind of the
Cane workers' machete
And in the eyes you see
The waves of the oceans
You see beads
Which form a necklace
Of islands
Which have emerged out of
The tears.

Apendeje

A Little Snake Over the

END

Victor Hernández Cruz was born in Aguas Buenas, Puerto Rico, in 1949, and was raised in New York City. His previous book publications include *Snaps* (Random House, 1969) *Mainland* (Random House, 1973), and *Tropicalization* (Reed, Cannon and Johnson, 1976). Since the early Seventies, Mr. Cruz has lived in San Francisco and is currently at work on a novel.

Book Design by Jon Goodchild. Cover art by Rupert Garcia. Phototypeset in Bembo by Sara Schrom, at Type By Design, Fairfax, California. Text preparation, selection and edit by Stephen Vincent, Harry Lewis, Gail Larrick, Beverly Dahlen, and Elisa I. Miranda.